DON'T
GIVE UP

JAKE & KEITH PROVANCE

WORD & SPIRIT
PUBLISHING

Don't Give Up
ISBN: 978-1-949106-67-1
Copyright © 2022 by Word and Spirit Publishing

Published by Word and Spirit Publishing
P.O. Box 701403
Tulsa, Oklahoma 74170
wordandspiritpublishing.com

Table of Contents

Introduction

Nobody may know why you are struggling today or why thoughts of giving up may be lingering in your mind. Perhaps the idea of quitting is just a passing thought, or maybe the idea has festered to the point that you feel at the end of your rope and you have lost all hope. Many issues in life can bring a person to their knees. It could be that you have experienced a life-altering event, like the death of a loved one, the diagnosis of a life-threatening disease, a divorce, or the threat of financial ruin. Maybe it's the betrayal of a close friend or a trusted coworker. Possibly you are the architect of your own demise, and your own actions of deceit and selfishness have alienated you from your family and friends. It could have been negligence on your part that has led to misfortune and pain in the lives of those whom you love the most. Maybe you have an addiction you cannot kick or repeated failures that have destroyed your self-confidence and left you living in a morass of discouragement and despair. Regardless of what has brought you to the brink of hopelessness, there is still hope—if you will grab hold of it. That hope is

Christ, and He can get you out of this mess if you let Him.

Like it or not, crises are normal to life in this world. This life is full of ups and downs, joys and sorrows, victories and defeats, grand accomplishments and heart-wrenching setbacks. Everything can be going great one day, and the next day the bottom can fall out and turn your life totally upside down. Being a Christian does not prevent us from experiencing these issues, but being a Christian gives us a hope and the stability to ride out the storm through faith. Though life on earth is ever-changing and nothing seems stable or certain, there is one thing that is certain, one thing that never changes, one thing you can always count on: Jesus. He will never leave you nor forsake you. His love for you is the one thing that will never change.

It may seem like God is a million miles away. You may feel like your prayers were never heard, and that God has simply given up on you. This could not be further from the truth. Nothing you have done or will do could ever be more powerful than what Jesus did for you. God's grace and mercy are ever constant and ferociously overtaking the sins of His children. All that is required is for us to ask for His help. There is light at the end of this tunnel, and with God's help, you can make it through. He has a plan to rescue you. No matter how deep of a pit you may be in, His love can pull you out. No matter how bad you have messed up or how deep in sin you might have fallen, His love is greater than your mistakes, failures, and shortcomings. You may feel that you are facing an insurmountable mountain that is just too big to get over. It might seem impossible, but I have good news—God specializes in the impossible! There is an answer, there is a path to victory, and there is hope. With God's help, you will get on the other side of this thing— whatever it is!

You must not give up. All is not lost; all hope is not gone. The night will not take you. The darkness will not claim you. Your past has not robbed you of your future. You are not out of options. Do not give up! The only way you will go no further in life is if you stop now. The only sure way to become a failure, for this to be the conclusion to your story instead of just a chapter in it, is by throwing in the towel and giving up.

You are not powerless to change. There is still untapped strength in you—a sleeping giant waiting to be awakened. You are not alone! There is a heaven on earth for you to enjoy, and a hell on earth for you to shun. There is a peace that passes all understanding ripe for the taking and an anxiousness for you to avoid. There is a hope for you to keep your eyes fixed upon and a worry for you to ignore. There is a love ready to transcend your highest dreams and a fear to overcome. But you must not give up!

This is not a lofty dream; this is God's wish for you! You have already tried life your way, and look where it has brought you! It is time to try something different. It is time to give God's way a chance.

He will come to your rescue and deliver you. He will provide a way of escape. Just cry out to Him, and He will answer you. By His Spirit and through His Word, you can find the help you need, the answers you are looking for, and the courage and strength to persevere and overcome even in the midst of the most adverse circumstances.

God is for you, God is with you, and He is on your side.

Our prayer for you is that as you read this book and meditate on the Scriptures here, the Lord will minister to you and show Himself strong on your behalf. We pray that His love surrounds you and engulfs you, and that His presence brings hope, healing, and encourage-ment to your heart.

"You don't have to see the whole staircase, just take the first step."

—MARTIN LUTHER KING JR.

Don't Give Up on Yourself

Disappointment, regret, and failure has affected all of us. If you have lived life on this earth for any amount of time, you will come to discover that no one has it all figured out.

Maybe you just don't believe in yourself anymore. Are you feeling that you have let your loved ones down, let your colleagues down, and let God down? It can feel like you have no place to retreat to, effectively immobilizing you with a web of discouragement, self-doubt, and apathy. When you lose faith in yourself, you stop trying, because you don't believe that things will ever change. Many of us have experienced what it is like to look in the mirror and see all our worst flaws, insecurities, and weaknesses. Although others would love for you to believe that they have all the answers and none of the problems, the truth is that no one but God fits that description.

So, don't let others' accomplishments or critical comments put you under condemnation. If you've messed up big-time, and often, then welcome to the club! God has not given up on you, so do not give up on yourself! God can restore your hope, fill your heart with His joy, fill your mind with His peace, and become your reason to live. Life has had and will have many challenges and obstacles for us to overcome. With God's help, we can choose to smile through the pain, press on through the confusion, and accomplish our God-given destiny. Conversely, we can also choose to break down in the midst of pain and confusion, making life a desperate attempt at survival. It is our perspective, our faith, and ultimately our choices that determine the life we will live.

So, it's time to let yourself off the hook and forgive yourself, because God already has! God has a plan and purpose for your life. Christianity is not the absence of problems; it's a relationship with our Creator, who gives us the strength, courage, and fortitude to carry on. He provides us with the tools and companionship to overcome all of life's difficulties. Do not let your past identify you and dictate your future. Let God define you and shape your future. The best part about it is, no matter how much we mess up, God tells us He will never leave us, never stop loving us, and forgive us any and every time we ask. Regardless of what you feel, or what you have done, it is time to believe in yourself again and refuse to give up!

Prayer

Lord, I know that I am a work in progress. Help me not to be so critical of myself. Help me to forgive myself for my sins and shortcomings, just like I know You have forgiven me. Help me to put the past behind me and focus on my life going forward. You know me better than anyone else—even better than I know myself. Help me to see myself as You see me. Help me to identify with what Your Word says I am in You. You say that I am fearfully and wonderfully made. You say that I am free, made new, redeemed from my mistakes, righteous in Your sight, loved, complete in You, chosen by You, strong because of You, a light in the darkness, an overcomer, more than a conqueror, protected by You, and most importantly, Your child. Let me believe these things over what my situation or other people say about me. Help me get to the point where my life reflects the truths of who I am according to Your Word. Show me how to find my identity in You and not in what I do. Help my focus and my motives to always be rooted in You. Thank You. In Jesus' name I pray, amen.

Scriptures

Therefore, since God in his mercy has given us this new way, we never give up.

—2 CORINTHIANS 4:1 (NLT)

Being confident of this very thing, that he which hath begun a good work in you will perform it until the day of Jesus Christ.

—PHILIPPIANS 1:6

I, even I, am He who blots out your transgressions for My own sake; And I will not remember your sins. Put Me in remembrance; Let us contend together; State your case, that you may be acquitted.

—ISAIAH 43:25-26 (NKJV)

Why art thou cast down, O my soul? And why art thou disquieted within me? Hope in God: For I shall yet praise him, Who is the health of my countenance, and my God.

—PSALM 43:5

There was a young lady who was demoted from her job as a news anchor because she *"wasn't fit for television."*

She went on to become one of television's highest-paid entertainers, producers, and actresses in her own television specials. That young lady is:

Oprah Winfrey.

"If God today told us what He's doing in the world, we wouldn't believe it. Don't you think God's given up and God's abdicated and God's left the throne. He hasn't! He's still on the throne, and those of us that know Him put our trust in Him and Him alone. I don't put my trust in Washington, I don't put my trust in the United Nations, I don't put my trust in myself, I don't put trust in my money, I put my trust in the Lord Jesus Christ. When all the rest of it fails and crumbles and shatters, He'll be there."

—BILLY GRAHAM

Don't Give Up on God

Don't give up on God, because He hasn't given up on you. God loves you. God is for you. God is on your side. God sent His Son, Jesus, to die on the cross just so He could adopt you into His family. It is never God's will for us to be in pain, sick, or lonely. God's desire is to see you happy and full of joy. It is God's desire to see you accomplishing your destiny with a sense of fulfillment and self-worth. It is God's desire to see you flourishing and at peace. God wants His children to be blessed! Sometimes we are tempted to blame God when things happen that we don't understand. The Bible makes it clear that we have an enemy that is against us. His plan is to kill, steal, and destroy anything good in your life. Jesus said He came that we might have life and have it more abundantly. It can be so easy for us to look at our lives and think that because we are in a difficult situation, it must mean God is upset with us or does not care about us. But God doesn't see us the way most of us see ourselves! God is not mad at you! Regardless of what you have done, God is ready and willing to forgive you, restore you, and help you accomplish your destiny if you would just ask!

In order for Him to help us, we must believe and have faith in what He has said. We must have more faith in what He said in the Bible than in what our circumstances are saying presently. Oftentimes, we give up our expectation of a better tomorrow because we experience hard times. We overcomplicate our relationship with God, and we begin to believe that the struggles we are experiencing are more "real" to us than God's love is. God never promised us a struggle-free or a problem-free life. He promised us His help to overcome the struggles and conquer our problems.

No matter how hard you get hit in life, always stay on God's side. God is the Source of our strength, our hope, our joy, our peace, and our life, and the worst thing we could do is forsake our trust in Him. Instead of blaming Him for your struggles, team up with Him and overcome your struggles!

Prayer

Lord, sometimes You seem far away. Sometimes it feels as if You do not hear my prayers. I know that You exist. I know that You love me. If I am being completely honest, however, I am struggling right now. I feel doubt creeping in about things I had once been so certain about. I know that faith is trusting You even when I do not sense Your presence. I am asking for Your grace and mercy concerning me. Help me to sense Your presence, to notice You and Your workings in my life daily, and to not be filled with so much doubt. I want to be close to You, to be the Christian whom I know I can be. I want to believe! I ask that You would make Your Word become progressively more real to me, so that I may know and understand, experientially, Your immeasurable love for me. There is no use in lying to You. You know that I have doubts, and I know that it takes faith to please You; so I am asking You to help me get to the place where my faith is big and my doubts are small, instead of the other way around. Fill my heart with Your joy and peace. Comfort and encourage me by Your Spirit. Make Yourself real to me. In Jesus' name I pray, amen.

Scriptures

Trust in the Lord, and do good; dwell in the land and befriend faithfulness. Delight yourself in the Lord, and he will give you the desires of your heart. Commit your way to the Lord; trust in him, and he will act. He will bring forth your righteousness as the light, and your justice as the noonday. Be still before the Lord and wait patiently for him; fret not yourself over the one who prospers in his way, over the man who carries out evil devices!

—PSALM 37:3-7 (ESV)

Teaching them to observe all things whatsoever I have commanded you: and, lo, I am with you always, even unto the end of the world. Amen.

—MATTHEW 28:20

For I am persuaded, that neither death, nor life, nor angels, nor principalities, nor powers, nor things present, nor things to come, nor height, nor depth, nor any other creature, shall be able to separate us from the love of God, which is in Christ Jesus our Lord.

—ROMANS 8:38-39

There was a young man wrongfully convicted. He would spend eighteen years of his sentence in Robben Island prison, which was known for its brutal treatment of the inmates and less than humane living conditions. Yet, he did not blame God for his difficulties; he chose to have faith and hope. He wrote in a letter to his wife, eleven years after being incarcerated, saying:

"Difficulties break some men but make others. No axe is sharp enough to cut the soul of a sinner who keeps on trying, one armed with the hope that he will rise even in the end."

This man was set free from his wrongful imprisonment after twenty-seven years. Many who knew him noted that he was a man of deep faith. With his faith still intact,

Nelson Mandela
became the President of South Africa.

"Part of being optimistic is keeping
one's head pointed toward the sun,
one's feet moving forward. There
were many dark moments when my
faith in humanity was sorely tested,
but I would not and could not give
myself up to despair. That way lays
defeat and death."

—NELSON MANDELA

Don't Give Up on Others

There is no pain quite like the pain of betrayal from a close friend, a spouse, or a family member. Betrayal is a devious thing. If we let down our walls and expose our hearts and innermost insecurities to someone, and they take advantage of that trust, it cuts us more deeply, in a way that nothing else can. It makes us feel like we are inadequate, left behind, undervalued, and replaced—like a tool to be used and disregarded. In the wake of betrayal, we experience waves of pain, hate, and the desire for them to feel the same pain that we have experienced. The betrayal can haunt us through life, causing us to obsess over it and leading us to be consumed with the "why" that makes the betrayal especially gruesome. We become withdrawn, discouraged, and depressed, and we build a wall around our heart a mile high, never to let anyone in again out of fear of what they might do. It becomes easy to be perpetually suspicious of the motives of others, even when their efforts of kindness and benevolence are sincere. When left unchecked, your suspicion grows into full-on cynicism, causing you to lose your faith in humanity altogether. So, how does one face betrayal, the fear in one's heart, and overcome the feeling that there is no kindness left in the world? The answer is simple: *forgiveness*.

You do not have the power to control the actions of others, but you do have the power to control how you will respond to those actions. Hate, unforgiveness, and cynicism act as a chain, tying you to the past. They doom you to relive the betrayal and see that betrayal everywhere.

Furthermore, in order to receive the Lord's help and receive deliverance from the hurt you are experiencing, you must forgive. Hate and unforgiveness are never the answer. The Bible tells us that unforgiveness hinders our prayers and hate paralyzes our faith. As impossible as it may seem to forgive someone who has purposely hurt or betrayed us, it is possible with the Lord's help, and it is an essential element to getting past the painful event. There is power in forgiveness to break the chains of hatred, resentment, and hurt and bring deliverance and freedom to your heart.

You can find comfort and peace in the Lord's presence and in His Word. You will find strength, confidence, and encouragement in His Word.

Prayer

Lord, help me to be quick to forgive others, just like You have forgiven me. Help me not to condemn or judge others, even when their actions have hurt me. Help me to love them and pray for them. Help me not to let the betrayal and deception of others cause me to become bitter or vengeful. Heal my heart, and help me not to be judgmental or cynical toward others in the future. By Your grace and through Your love, restore my soul. Help me to let Your love, light, and life shine through me to those around me. Finally, help me to move on from the past and enjoy a wonderful life in You. In Jesus' name I pray, amen.

Scriptures

And be ye kind one to another, tender-hearted, forgiving one another, even as God for Christ's sake hath forgiven you.

—EPHESIANS 4:32

Bearing with one another, and forgiving one another, if anyone has a complaint against another; even as Christ forgave you, so you also must do.

—COLOSSIANS 3:13 (NKJV)

He did not retaliate when he was insulted, nor threaten revenge when he suffered. He left his case in the hands of God, who always judges fairly.

—1 PETER 2:23 (NLT)

Judge not, and ye shall not be judged: condemn not, and ye shall not be condemned: forgive, and ye shall be forgiven.

—LUKE 6:37

But I say unto you, Love your enemies, bless them that curse you, do good to them that hate you, and pray for them which despitefully use you, and persecute you.

—MATTHEW 5:44

There was a lady who had to live through the Holocaust. She had to endure terrible acts of atrocity from the hands of her captors at the concentration camp known as Ravensbruck. One of these atrocities was watching her sister die. Later, she would come back to a defeated Germany and preach to the people about love and forgiveness. A man pushed through the crowd towards the front, and as he stood there before the lady, she recognized him as one of the guards from the camp. He had since become a Christian and held out his hand to her and asked if she would forgive him. Her response:

"Still I stood there with the coldness clutching my heart. But forgiveness is not an emotion—I knew that too. Forgiveness is an act of the will, and the will can function regardless of the temperature of the heart. 'Jesus, help me!' I prayed silently. 'I can lift my hand, I can do that much. You supply the feeling.' And so woodenly, mechanically, I thrust my hand into the one stretched out to me. And as I did, an incredible thing took place . . . I had never known God's love so intensely as I did then."

—CORRIE TEN BOOM

"Never give up on what you really want to do. The person with big dreams is more powerful than the one with all the facts."

—Albert Einstein

Don't Give Up on Your Dreams

When we were young, we all had big dreams. For many, though, somewhere along the bumpy road of life, those dreams took a back seat to the issues of living. With each passing year, those dreams fade, until eventually we give up on them altogether. Many young men and women dream of becoming movie stars, athletes, astronauts, wealthy entrepreneurs, and so on. And although there is nothing wrong with those dreams, as Christians, the question we should be asking is what dream does God have for us. We should grow out of dreams rooted in the pursuit of riches and fame and grow into the dreams we foster through our relationship with God! God made you, and He put the perfect gifts and personality together in you to meet a specific need in the world. The only way to discover what you were made to do is to go directly to the Source and ask Him! Once you know what God has destined you for, then comes the challenge of holding on to that dream with faith, hope, and determination.

Regardless of your age, your station, or the path you have walked up to this point, God has not changed His mind about what He has destined you to do. So many in this world have searched and searched for meaning, purpose, and "inner peace," only to come up utterly short. They are looking in the world for what can only be found in God. God made you, and He had a dream for your life before you did. And He wants to see you flourishing, full of joy, purpose, and peace. He wants you and Him to accomplish great things for the Kingdom, working in tandem together.

So, whether your passion for fulfilling your dream has grown cold, or you have yet to discover what truly makes you come alive, God has the key to bringing those dreams into reality. He knows exactly what will make you the happiest and the most fulfilled. His dreams and plans are good and for your benefit, never for your detriment. Don't allow petty excuses to stand between you and your dream; God will provide the resources, contacts, and favor that you need to accomplish it. God is in your corner, and He will provide you with the courage, strength, and fortitude to keep going. So, look to Him, even when your dreams look further away than ever, and He will bring them to pass. Quit chasing after money, power, and influence. These pursuits will taint your dream. Instead, chase after God and His pleasure, and you will realize your dream.

Prayer

Lord, I ask You to reveal Your plan and purpose for my life. Not my will, but Your will be done, in every area of my life. Thank You, Lord, for placing gifts and talents inside of me. I ask that You would help me to recognize and utilize those gifts and talents—to bring into fruition the purpose that You have set for me. I pray for the courage and the strength to weather the storms that may crash into my dreams. I ask for the wisdom to discern the things that I should remove from my life because they are acting as hindrances to Your plan and purpose. Show me the things that I should do daily to help further Your plan and to help develop the gifts and talents You've placed inside me. I pray for divine contacts and supernatural favor so that I may accomplish the dreams that You have placed in my heart. Finally, I ask that You would help me keep my attention focused on my future instead of on my past, and on You instead of all the reasons why my dreams could never come true. All things are possible through You, and I thank You for my dreams coming true! In Jesus' name I pray, amen.

Scriptures

But Jesus beheld them, and said unto them, With men this is impossible; but with God all things are possible.

—MATTHEW 19:26

"For I know the plans and thoughts that I have for you," says the Lord, "plans for peace and well-being and not for disaster, to give you a future and a hope."

—JEREMIAH 29:11 (AMP)

So Jesus said to them, "Because of your unbelief; for assuredly, I say to you, if you have faith as a mustard seed, you will say to this mountain, 'Move from here to there,' and it will move; and nothing will be impossible for you."

—MATTHEW 17:20 (NKJV)

Jesus looked hard at them and said, "No chance at all if you think you can pull it off yourself. Every chance in the world if you trust God to do it."

—MATTHEW 19:26 (MSG)

There was a young cartoonist fired from a newspaper for:

"lacking imagination" and *"having no original ideas."*

He would later try and fail many times, resulting in embarrassment and bankruptcy. He even contemplated suicide, but he had a dream bigger than himself, and would do anything to make that dream a reality. Keeping his dream out in front of him, he eventually would become a household name and create an entire enterprise built on pure imagination. When asked about his success in his later years, he responded with:

*"All our **dreams** can come true, if we have the courage to pursue them." "If you can visualize it, if you can **dream** it, there's some way to do it."*

—WALT DISNEY

"Far better it is to dare mighty things, to win glorious triumphs, even though checkered by failure, than to take rank with those poor spirits who neither enjoy much nor suffer much, because they live in the gray twilight that knows neither victory nor defeat."

—TEDDY ROOSEVELT

Don't Give Up before You Start

The unfortunate truth is that many people will never accomplish anything significant for the Kingdom in their lives. This is not due to a lack of connections, resources, or ability. It is simply because they never began. They gave up before they started.

Some of the brightest minds, the greatest athletes, and the most talented performers will never be known, simply because they lacked the courage to start. They have tried and failed, listened to small-minded naysayers, bought into the lie of how "unlikely" their dream was to succeed, or fallen on hard times and had to push their dream aside until it remains only as a reminder of what could have been. The truly famous minds, athletes, and performers are known simply because they were committed to their dream and refused to give up on it.

You'll end up regretting the things you never did far more than the things that you did.

Don't let past failures deter you from trying again. Don't for one second think that your age, abilities, health, or financial situation can stop you from making a difference in this world. If you have even the smallest hint in your heart to do something for the Kingdom, do it! God is with you, and He'll help you, but He can't make you start. Step out in faith, and step into a life of dependency on God. Write that book, start that business, learn a different language, go on a mission trip, travel to that country that you've always wanted to visit—whatever the desire may be that God has placed in your heart to do, do it! One of the things that Jesus' disciples prayed for constantly was boldness. They felt the pressure that a lack of finances presents, along with persecution from governmental and religious figures and harsh criticism from others. They needed courage, confidence, and boldness to step out and do what God told them to do. So, if you are scared and insecure about starting to step outside your comfort zone while endeavoring to do something for God, then you are in good company! Having courage is not the absence of fear, but the triumph over it. So, even if you are afraid and have doubts, do it anyway—step out in faith and watch God show Himself strong on your behalf. Where you lack resources, God will provide. Where you lack wisdom, ask and He will give of it liberally. Your job is to start, and then trust God to guide and empower you until you see the fulfillment of your God-given desires.

Prayer

Father, I ask for the confidence to step out in the pursuit of the plans and the purposes You have destined for my life. I ask for the boldness to accomplish my God-given destiny. I ask for clarity and wisdom concerning the direction I should go. If I am going to take a step of faith, I first have to know where to step. I want to step where You tell me to; I do not want to step out in my own strength and fail.

Help me to be keen to hear and quick to obey the leading of Your Spirit in all of my endeavors. Help me to make good and godly decisions. Help me to never compromise my convictions or my integrity in my quest for success. Help me to stay focused on Your will and not my own will and desires. I ask You to provide the necessary favor, finances, and freedom to accomplish all that You have destined me to accomplish in this life. In Jesus' name I pray, amen.

Scriptures

Finally, my brethren, be strong in the Lord, and in the power of his might.

—EPHESIANS 6:10

For God hath not given us the spirit of fear; but of power, and of love, and of a sound mind.

—2 TIMOTHY 1:7

Wherefore seeing we also are compassed about with so great a cloud of witnesses, let us lay aside every weight, and the sin which doth so easily beset us, and let us run with patience the race that is set before us.

—HEBREWS 12:1

There was a young boy who wasn't able to speak until he was almost four years old. When he began attending school, he would have a teacher tell him that he would, "never amount to much." It would have been incredibly easy for this young man to quit school and never have anything to do with it ever again. Instead, even with what many considered a disadvantage,

Albert Einstein *continued down the path of academia and is known worldwide for his intelligence.*

"Most of the important things in the world have been accomplished by people who have kept on trying when there seemed to be no hope at all."

—Dale Carnegie

Don't Give Up When Addicted

An addiction can be one of the most destructive things in a person's life. It might be an addiction to alcohol, nicotine, drugs, pornography, excessive eating, or a myriad of other things. It can be hidden, or obvious, but it is never without its destructive nature. Accepting its destructive nature is not the issue that we face when fighting this foe; we feel desperate and helpless when we try to overcome our addictions. You may have read every book you could find, prayed a thousand prayers, joined support groups, and done everything else you could think of. Or you may be in the midst of an internal war, living a double life in which you feel more isolated with every relationship and every positive interaction, because they are trying to connect with who you are pretending to be. Guilt and shame become your constant companions, and you may feel as if you have let everyone down—including God. This is the sad reality of someone who struggles with addiction. Eventually, all who struggle with such things come to the same conclusion: "I can't beat this thing."

I have good news for you: You are right! Alone, you are powerless to overcome addiction, but the good news is that you don't have to fight it alone anymore. Christ paid for your freedom on the cross, and regardless of how often you have given in to your addiction, how much destruction has resulted because of your poor choices, and how hypocritical you might feel asking for God's forgiveness for the thousandth time, you still cannot exhaust God's goodness, mercy, and love. He will give you a fresh start every morning! This is only one chapter in your story, and while it may feel like a long chapter at that, the next chapter is victory! The weaker we feel and the more mistakes we make, the greater our desire to run from the only Person who can really help us: our Father, God. Do not allow shame and condemnation to hang on you and create distance between you and God. Choose to smile, laugh, and enjoy life in faith that what Christ has done is more powerful than what you have done. Lastly, renew your mind. Addiction has a way of making all our thoughts revolve around it. So, in order to win against it, we must replace the centerpiece of our thought life. We need our thoughts to revolve around Christ. Don't give up—you've got this!

Prayer

Thank You, Lord, for loving me, even when I fail or come short. I thank You that Your grace and loving-kindness are new every morning. I thank You that nothing can separate me from Your love, not even my own failures and mistakes. Lord, I need Your help. I admit that I cannot beat this addiction on my own. I have tried and failed over and over. I am humbly asking for Your help. Give me the strength, the courage, and the fortitude to make the changes that I need to make. I know that nothing is impossible with You. Your Word says that when I am weak, then Your strength will sustain me. Help me to make the right decisions and stand strong in You. Your Word says that greater is He that is in me than he that is in the world. Help me to lean on Your Spirit in me to overcome temptation and say no to my self-destructive behavior. Your Word says that I can do all things through You. Help me to trust and rely on You, thus gaining the courage to rise above this addiction. In Jesus' name I pray, amen.

Scriptures

But I need something more! For if I know the law but still can't keep it, and if the power of sin within me keeps sabotaging my best intentions, I obviously need help! I realize that I don't have what it takes. I can will it, but I can't do it. I decide to do good, but I don't really do it; I decide not to do bad, but then I do it anyway. My decisions, such as they are, don't result in actions. Something has gone wrong deep within me and gets the better of me every time. It happens so regularly that it's predictable. The moment I decide to do good, sin is there to trip me up. I truly delight in God's commands, but it's pretty obvious that not all of me joins in that delight. Parts of me covertly rebel, and just when I least expect it, they take charge. I've tried everything and nothing helps. I'm at the end of my rope. Is there no one who can do anything for me? Isn't that the real question? The answer, thank God, is that Jesus Christ can and does. He acted to set things right in this life of contradictions where I want to serve God with all my heart and mind, but am pulled by the influence of sin to do something totally different.

—The Apostle Paul
ROMANS 7:17-25 (MSG)

There was a poor cotton farmer that desired to be a famous musician. He set out to make his mark through the rockabilly scene in Memphis, Tennessee. Despite his situation, and against all odds, his career started to take off in the late 1950s. Sadly, he started drinking heavily and became addicted to amphetamines and barbiturates. The rapid decline of his mental health, emotional stability, and his ability to perform were all evident. He felt hopeless as his life fell apart. However, with the love of his family, he came back to the Lord and finally broke free of his addiction. He rose to incredible fame. He later commented on his stint with drugs saying:

"I have tried drugs and a little of everything else, and there is nothing in the world more soul-satisfying than having the Kingdom of God building inside you and growing."

—Johnny Cash

"You gain strength, courage, and confidence by every experience in which you really stop to look fear in the face. You are able to say to yourself, 'I lived through this horror. I can take the next thing that comes along.'"

—ELEANOR ROOSEVELT

Don't Give Up When Facing a Crisis

Unfortunately, whether we like it or not, crises are normal to life. All of us from time to time will be faced with a major crisis in our lives. It may be the loss of a job, a bitter divorce, financial failure, a major illness, or the death of a loved one. When relationships, financial security, or things that you have spent a lifetime of blood, sweat, and tears to accumulate are suddenly gone, the prospect of repeating the journey can be so daunting, and in some cases, seem impossible. It can force the strongest of us to our knees, contemplating the great taboo of giving up. Crises can rattle us to the core, causing us to question our own abilities, spirituality, faith, and usefulness. Anxiety, worry, and fear seem to stalk our thought life, and if they are left unchecked, we can easily slide into deep depression and check out mentally.

So, what do we do when our back is up against the wall, when we are faced with impossible odds, and when the solution is nowhere in sight? We look to God.

God loves you, and He is willing to help you if you ask. Have faith in God. Faith is acting on God's Word even when you do not feel like it. Do not let your feelings control your actions. Faith is praising God for your deliverance when it looks helpless. He is a very present help in times of trouble, and all of those who look to Him will never be put to shame or left without support. We can receive His peace when we feel scared, His wisdom to navigate us through the confusion, His love to quiet our insecurities, and His joy when we are wearied and overwhelmed. Crises are not something that a Christian should fear. We are not immune to crises, but with the Lord's help, we can and will make it through the storms of life. So, turn to God when you feel like giving up, right there in the midst of your crisis. Refocus your attention from how big the problem is to how big our God is. Keep your attention fixed on what God said He would do, and not what the situation threatens to do. At every turn, keep your gaze fixed on Christ, and His perfect peace will see you through to the other side of the crisis unharmed.

Prayer

Lord, I ask for Your help. Right now, my situation is speaking so loudly that it is hard to hear much of anything else. The waves of life have crashed so hard into my reality that I feel unsteady, shaken, and rattled to the core. I know that You are good and that You love me, and yet the crisis at hand seems to speak only of pain and difficulties. Help me learn how to place my complete trust in You. I ask that You would pierce through this darkness and reach me with Your hope. You know I want the tragedy to end and be over with, but more importantly, I want You. I want Your peace, Your joy, Your love, Your hope, and Your friendship. You said in Your Word that You would never leave me nor forsake me. I trust and believe in what You have said. Give me the strength, the courage, and the endurance to not give up. Help me put my total faith and confidence in You, knowing that You will see me through. In Jesus' name I pray, amen.

Scriptures

God keeps track of the decent folk; what they do won't soon be forgotten. In hard times, they'll hold their heads high; when the shelves are bare, they'll be full.

—PSALM 37:18-19 (MSG)

These things I have spoken unto you, that in me ye might have peace. In the world ye shall have tribulation: but be of good cheer; I have overcome the world.

—JOHN 16:33

Many are the afflictions of the righteous: but the Lord delivereth him out of them all.

—PSALM 34:19

I know how to be abased and live humbly in straitened circumstances, and I know also how to enjoy plenty and live in abundance. I have learned in any and all circumstances the secret of facing every situation, whether well-fed or going hungry, having a sufficiency and enough to spare or going without and being in want. I have strength for all things in Christ Who empowers me. I am ready for anything and equal to anything through Him Who infuses inner strength into me; I am self-sufficient in Christ's sufficiency.

—PHILIPPIANS 4:12-13 (AMPC)

See It Through

When you're up against a trouble,
Meet it squarely, face to face;
Lift your chin and set your shoulders,
Plant your feet and take a brace.
When it's vain to try to dodge it,
Do the best that you can do;
You may fail, but you may conquer,
See it through!

Black may be the clouds about you
And your future may seem grim,
But don't let your nerve desert you;
Keep yourself in fighting trim.
If the worst is bound to happen,
Spite of all that you can do,
Running from it will not save you,
See it through!

Even hope may seem but futile,
When with troubles you're beset,
But remember you are facing
Just what other men have met.
You may fail, but fall still fighting;
Don't give up, whate'er you do;
Eyes front, head high to the finish.
See it through!

—EDGAR ALBERT GUEST

"We have always held to the hope,
the belief, the conviction that there
is a better life, a better world,
beyond the horizon."

—FRANKLIN D. ROOSEVELT

Don't Give Up When You Feel Suicidal

If you have exhausted all your options, and giving up seems to be the only choice that you have left; if things feel as if they will never change, and you feel helpless and hopeless at the same time; if you feel like you've lost control over your life, and you question if it is even worth living—if you have ever felt these things, then you know what it is like to feel trapped. It is an unfortunate truth that many will find themselves feeling helpless, hopeless, and alone in a room with no doors. They feel like they have only two options left to them: endure the torment a bit longer or give in to the despair and commit suicide. But suicide is never the answer! Suicide does not end your pain; it takes the pain, multiplies it, and then spreads it to all of those closest to you. Nobody in your life would be better off without you in it. Even if you feel a desperate cry to be heard, noticed, and loved, ending your life cannot give you any of these things. Death has no good purpose. There is another way. There is a third option in the doorless room of despair for you to take. Instead of trying to escape through suicide, you can let somebody else into the room with you. Quit fighting alone! God sent His beloved Son to die for you, and He eagerly wishes to hear from you. He is the One you have been looking for. You do not have to feel helpless any longer. Your hope for a sunny tomorrow does not have to be foundationless dreaming. All you have to do is cry out right there in the middle of your mess. Chemical imbalances, abuse, poor choices, or a thousand other things could have played a role in your current predicament, but there is one path to take for your restoration: crying out to your Father God for love and help. This doesn't mean you should not seek therapy or medicinal help. God uses people and medicine to help us when we need it. These things complement the truth of God's love for you and His desire for you to be happy, fulfilled, and at peace. Your emotions may not level out in a day. People may still be petty toward you. You may feel at times that you are right back where you started. But don't lose hope. Keep praying, keep believing, keep reading the Word of God, and keep moving forward!

Prayer

Father, You know my heart, You see my desires, and You see my insecurities—You see me. Of all the people in this world, there is only One who truly knows me inside and out, and that's You. You made me, and You have adopted me into Your family. I know there is nothing that is impossible to You, and because of Your great love for me, I know that You are not only able, but You are willing to help me. I feel trapped, helpless, and hopeless all at the same time by my current situation. Full disclosure, Father: I've fallen into a deep hole that I can't seem to get out of. I've struggled and tried to get out, but it has reached the point where I have no idea how I will ever feel hope, purpose, or real freedom again. In Your Word, You said that You would always provide a way of escape for me, no matter how desperate the circumstance. I'm asking for Your fatherly help. I don't have to know how to escape or how to make it all okay—because I know You do. You are my refuge. You are my shelter. I trust You. Thank You, Father. In Jesus' name I pray, amen.

Scriptures

What is the value of your soul to God? Could your worth be defined by any amount of money? God doesn't abandon or forget even the small sparrow he has made. How then could he forget or abandon you? What about the seemingly minor issues of your life? Do they matter to God? Of course they do! So you never need to worry, for you are more valuable to God than anything else in this world.

—LUKE 12:6-7 (TPT)

Therefore, since God in his mercy has given us this new way, we never give up.

—2 CORINTHIANS 4:1 (NLT)

For we do not have a High Priest Who is unable to understand and sympathize and have a shared feeling with our weaknesses and infirmities and liability to the assaults of temptation, but One Who has been tempted in every respect as we are, yet without sinning. Let us then fearlessly and confidently and boldly draw near to the throne of grace (the throne of God's unmerited favor to us sinners), that we may receive mercy for our failures and find grace to help in good time for every need, appropriate help and well-timed help, coming just when we need it.

—HEBREWS 4:15-16 (AMPC)

There was a young Missouri boy who decided that he would become a novelist. Like many who have such dreams and desires, he found himself working for various newspapers and contributing towards an article or two. His lack of success became part of his trademark satire. Though he joked quite often, he was in deep poverty and in deep pain on the inside. He wrote a letter to his brother, saying that if things don't improve, he is going to end his own life. He was desperate, but he chose to resist the urge to commit suicide and kept fighting for his dream. He ended up writing over twenty books, selling millions of copies, becoming a humorist, entrepreneur, publisher, and lecturer. He would have never realized the life he could have lived if he would have given into despair—and the world would have missed something very special and unique.

Mark Twain
is still celebrated around the world
for his literary contributions.

"Failure should be our teacher, not
our undertaker. Failure is delay, not
defeat. It is a temporary detour, not
a dead end. Failure is something we
can avoid only by saying nothing,
doing nothing, and being nothing."

—DENIS WAITLEY

Don't Give Up When You Fail

Failing is an inescapable part of the human experience. We all get knocked down from time to time, but just because you have failed, that does not make you a failure. Every successful person in history who has achieved anything worthwhile has experienced a long list of failures. But they refused to give up, even when faced with devastating circumstances, even when they had lost everything, even when it looked like there was no hope. What made them stand out in the annals of history was their perseverance through defeat. They refused to personalize their failures, they refused to let failure define them, and they were able to learn from their failures.

Your failures say you can't, but God says that with Him you *can*. Your failures say that you are a failure, but God says that you are an overcomer. Your failures say it's too late, but God says that He's not done with you yet! God takes the sting out of failure and the finality out of defeat. With God, you always have one more chance to make a difference. Do not let the fear of another failure deter you! Failures can be pivotal experiences that either break your spirit, or they can act as stepping-stones on your way to victory. This is to be every Christian's testimony, for this is the testimony of faith. If we fail, God forgives; when we are weak, God becomes our strength; when we feel alone, God reminds us of His presence; and when we don't see a way out, God says that He will make a way where there seems to be no way. Sometimes past failures are like a ball and chain shackled to your soul. Sometimes you may forget that it is there until you try to take a step forward. It takes faith to get back up after a failure, to believe that God is greater than any mistake. You can count on this:

His love will sustain you, and His favor will open new doors of opportunity for you if you persevere and refuse to quit.

It pleases Him to see His children dust themselves off after failures, to put their trust in Him, and to be determined to go forward in faith, knowing that the Lord will sustain, strengthen, and guide them toward their destiny. So, it is time to grit our teeth and press on, even in the face of adversity. And it is time to always, with undaunted courage, keep moving forward with a fierce faith and a determination that with God's help we will fulfill our divine destiny.

Prayer

Lord, I've done it again. I have failed. What are You to do with someone like me? How is it that You say such different things about me in Your Word than what seems to be true? Why are You filled with such unfailing love toward me when all I do is fall short and in error again and again? Thank You for Your kindness and mercy toward Your children. I ask for Your mercy now. I know You do not see me as a failure. Help me not to see myself that way as well. Help me to see myself the way that You see me. Help me to dust myself off and move forward from here. I ask that our relationship would grow through all of this. Even when I fail, even when I fall short, I always know that You are there to pick me up. Help me to forget the past and move forward in faith. Help me to learn from my mistakes without letting those mistakes dominate my thoughts. Help me to focus on the future instead of lamenting over the past. Lead me in all my endeavors, so that I may bring glory to You. In Jesus' name I pray, amen.

Scriptures

The steps of a good man are ordered by the Lord: and he delighteth in his way. Though he fall, he shall not be utterly cast down: for the Lord upholdeth him with his hand.

—PSALM 37:23-24

Rejoice not against me, O mine enemy: when I fall, I shall arise; when I sit in darkness, the Lord shall be a light unto me.

—MICAH 7:8

For a just man falleth seven times, and riseth up again: But the wicked shall fall into mischief.

—PROVERBS 24:16

No, dear brothers and sisters, I have not achieved it, but I focus on this one thing: Forgetting the past and looking forward to what lies ahead, I press on to reach the end of the race and receive the heavenly prize for which God, through Christ Jesus, is calling us.

—PHILIPPIANS 3:13-14 (NLT)

There was a famous politician who pushed through a lot more failures than people realize. In 1831, this man lost his job. In 1832, he was defeated in his run for Illinois State Legislature. In 1833, he tried his hand at business, only to fail miserably. In 1835, his sweetheart died. In 1836, he had a nervous breakdown. In 1838, he was defeated in the run for Illinois House Speaker. In 1843, he was defeated in the run for the nomination to be in the U.S. Congress. In 1846, he finally caught a break and was elected to Congress—only to lose reelection just two years later. He went on to lose renomination and was rejected for a land officer position. Over the next ten years, he would go on to lose twice when running for the senate, and also lose in a nomination for becoming the Vice President. After just about thirty years of heart-wrenching failure,

Abraham Lincoln
was elected President in 1860.

"Never give in, never give in, never, never, never, never—in nothing, great or small, large or petty—never give in except to convictions of honor and good sense. Never yield to force; never yield to the apparently overwhelming might of the enemy."

—WINSTON CHURCHILL

Don't Give Up When Pressured

We all have to deal with various pressures in our lives: The pressure to perform at work or at home. The pressure to fit in and the pressure to stand out. The pressure to be successful or to provide for a family. A certain amount of pressure is common to everyone. However, there is a pressure that is so intense that we feel like we just cannot take it anymore. It can be a sudden event that threatens to crush us with overwhelming force. It could be the death of a loved one, a divorce, or losing your vocation and life's work that has left you on the roadside of despair. There is also a steady rise in the pent-up stress, anxiety, discontentment, and the feeling of falling behind in life that causes our journey to seem too difficult to continue. It's when we reach our physical limit, our financial limit, and our emotional limit, and life's demands remain ceaseless and our situation hopeless, that we all want to give up. It is this type of unrelenting pressure that has brought the strongest to their knees. With enough pressure put on anyone or anything, eventually something has to give. It may end up being at home, at work, or when we are with our friends, but unless we can deal with the pressure, it's only a matter of time before something in our life blows up.

No matter how dark the night, no matter how deep the pit of despair, no matter how hopeless it might seem, there is *always* a way out and *always* a reason not to give up. His name is Jesus. Jesus said to come to Him when you are burdened down and He will give you rest. Jesus said to cast your cares on Him because He cares about you. He loves you unconditionally. Take your weariness, your pain, your worries, your confusion, your hopelessness, and everything that has been weighing you down, and lay it all at His feet. The pressure in our lives only grows when we are constantly focusing on the situation. However, God's peace grows in our lives when we keep our thoughts and attention focused on Him. So, listen to praise and worship music, pray, read the Bible, and listen to sermons regularly—except when the pressures of life become intense. Then you should listen, pray, and read all the more fervently. Keep your attention on how big God is, and the pressure of your situation will diminish while your faith in God and your peace will grow.

Prayer

Lord, there is so much pressure in my life right now. It seems unrelenting and unending, with no obvious hope of letting up. Without Your help, I do not see how I can stand it much longer. But with Your help, I know I can make it. Help me to cast my cares on You and trust You completely. Help me to find that place of refuge, that place of calmness and peace that can only be found in You, that place where the cares, worries, and pressures of this life fade away in the glory of Your presence. Help me not to let the pressure of the moment force me into making an ill-fated decision I will later regret. Give me wisdom and clarity of thought to properly discern the choices available to me. Let me not be agitated, disturbed, or intimidated by the circumstances around me. Grant me Your peace so that I may maintain calm in the midst of adversity. I ask You for Your guidance and direction concerning the choices before me. Lord, I trust You and will follow Your direction, wherever You may lead. In Jesus' name I pray, amen.

Scriptures

But that's not all! Even in times of trouble we have a joyful confidence, knowing that our pressures will develop in us patient endurance. And patient endurance will refine our character, and proven character leads us back to hope. And this hope is not a disappointing fantasy, because we can now experience the endless love of God cascading into our hearts through the Holy Spirit who lives in us!

—ROMANS 5:3-5 (TPT)

We are hedged in (pressed) on every side, troubled and oppressed in every way, but not cramped or crushed; we suffer embarrassments and are perplexed and unable to find a way out, but not driven to despair; We are pursued (persecuted and hard driven), but not deserted to stand alone; we are struck down to the ground, but never struck out and destroyed.

—2 CORINTHIANS 4:8-9 (AMPC)

Watch, stand fast in the faith, be brave, be strong.

—1 CORINTHIANS 16:13 (NKJV)

There was a young man who faced incredible pressure and persecution. He was arrested over twenty times for protesting. He was the object of several violent attacks, both to his person and his property. He received threatening phone calls, his home was bombed and set afire, and he was even stabbed. He endured all of this for the sake of his unwillingness to yield or buckle to the pressures of the world. He had a dream, and though many would pressure him to make that dream violent, while others tried to silence him by any means necessary, he still persevered through the pressure to deliver his dream of equality to the world:

"I have a dream that one day every valley shall be exalted, and every hill and mountain shall be made low. The rough places will be plain, and the crooked places will be made straight, and the glory of the Lord shall be revealed, and all flesh shall see it together."

—MARTIN LUTHER KING JR.

"God does not dispense strength and encouragement like a druggist fills your prescription. The Lord doesn't promise to give us something to take so we can handle our weary moments. He promises us Himself. That is all. And that is enough."

—CHARLES R. SWINDOLL

Don't Give Up When You Become Weary

We all feel weary from time to time. It is part of the human experience. Society has progressively become busier and more fast-paced, which only adds to this condition. For the most part, a good night's sleep, a day off from work, or a cup of coffee can refresh us and get us back on track. But there is a weariness that goes much deeper. This is the kind of weariness you cannot sleep off. It seems to follow you wherever you go, like a nagging heaviness that you cannot escape. Your mind becomes fatigued, your strength of will fades, and your emotions are drained. In short, the physical weakness that doesn't dissipate with sleep is the result of a weary soul. Our mind, will, and emotions play an incredible role in our lives, and when we gather our strength from the wrong sources, we are doomed to run out of steam sooner or later. Sometimes the same things that once drove us now act as anchors around our necks. Too often, we don't realize how bad of a state we are in until it becomes a struggle even to get out of bed in the morning. This is because weariness is a slow fall, a gradual decline of our mental and emotional health, until we wake up one morning completely void of any strength, peace, joy, or hope. Many of us slip into the trap of trying to gain our validation and fulfillment through outside sources when we are meant to gain these through Christ. Jesus said:

"Come to Me all you who are burdened and I will give you rest."

Could you use a real rest? Come to Christ!

He created you, and He knows exactly what He put in you. He knows how to draw out your potential, to set you ablaze with a contagious passion, to fill your heart with a love so pure and genuine that you would never need to seek it from anywhere else ever again. It was His design and His desire to commune with you, to lead you, and to show you purpose. Fellowship with Him daily. He's with you, He hears you, and He will sustain you. He is easily touched with what affects your life. Cast your cares on Him, and look to Him. God loves you, cares for you, and desires for you to live a joyful, carefree, and fulfilled life, free from weariness and the worries of this life.

Prayer

Father, I come to You in need of Your help. You said in Your Word, "Come to Me, all you who are weary and burdened down, and I will give you rest." That is what I am doing right now. I am coming to You to ask for Your help. The struggles and challenges of my life have taken their toll. I am weary and battle-worn. Sometimes it feels like I do not have the mental and physical strength to make it another day. I need Your help. I cast all my cares, worries, and fears on You. Restore my soul, fill my heart with Your joy, fill my mind with Your peace, and give me the strength to endure and the courage to press on. Comfort me with Your loving arms. Hold me close. Refresh my soul with Your love. Let Your mercy and goodness give me assurance that You will never leave me or abandon me in my time of need. Help me to put my complete trust in You. In Jesus' name I pray, amen.

Scriptures

He gives power to the faint and weary, and to him who has no might He increases strength causing it to multiply and making it to abound. Even youths shall faint and be weary, and selected young men shall feebly stumble and fall exhausted; But those who wait for the Lord, who expect, look for, and hope in Him, shall change and renew their strength and power; they shall lift their wings and mount up close to God as eagles, mount up to the sun; they shall run and not be weary, they shall walk and not faint or become tired.

—Isaiah 40:29-31 (AMPC)

So let's not get tired of doing what is good. At just the right time we will reap a harvest of blessing if we don't give up.

—Galatians 6:9 (NLT)

To appoint unto them that mourn in Zion, to give unto them beauty for ashes, the oil of joy for mourning, the garment of praise for the spirit of heaviness; that they might be called trees of righteousness, the planting of the Lord, that he might be glorified.

—Isaiah 61:3

There was a young boy who loved to sing and dance. He started when he was very young and followed that passion his whole life. After working hard for over twenty years, he would receive some of the toughest criticism from a studio executive in the area of his dreams.

During his first screen test, the executive wrote:

"Can't sing. Can't act. Balding. Can dance a little."

His entire life's pursuit was crushed. He finds out from the people who matter the most when it comes to performing on the big screen in the job of his dreams, that he simply didn't have what it takes. It would have been easy for anyone to throw in the towel. But instead, it is said that this man hung up that note from the executive on his wall as motivation.

So, despite this initial rejection,

Fred Astaire
persevered and ended up becoming one of the top actors, singers, and dancers of his generation.

"The marvelous richness of human experience would lose something of rewarding joy if there were no limitations to overcome. The hilltop hour would not be half so wonderful if there were no dark valleys to traverse."

—HELEN KELLER

Don't Give Up on the Fight

When the waves of life have crashed relentlessly over your dreams, and your resolve, conviction, and passion gradually erode with each wave, it can be easy to think that you do not have what it takes to make a difference anymore. You start to believe lies about yourself, and about what stands in-between you and your destiny. The folly of your poor decisions and wrong priorities may have left you feeling defeated and nurturing a victim mentality. And if this were the end of your story, then it would be a tragedy indeed. But this is *not* the end of your story; this is only a chapter in it. And although you may feel insignificant, and you may want to give up, something in you whispers, "Get back up and give it all you've got."

That something is the Spirit of God! God has not abandoned you, and He never will. While you draw breath, there is hope for you! What time and circumstances have eroded, His love will restore. You may not be able to solve all your problems in one day. But you can make a decision that puts you on the path that will lead you out. That is the decision to fight back. Fight back against discouragement, fear, and anxiety. It is time to rise above the pity party of self-doubt and condemnation. It's time to get past the past and move forward. It's time to rise up with a determined spirit and fulfill what God has destined you to accomplish. Quit waiting around for someone else to discover you, for someone else to believe in you, and for someone else to make your dreams a reality. God sees you and believes in you. He wants to see you realize your destiny more than you do! It's not time to lie down. It's time to get up and fight. It is time to push back. The Bible tells us to fight the good fight of faith. How do we do that? By putting our trust in God and acting on His Word. By believing that God is for us and will never forsake us, believing that He will help us to fulfill the plan and purpose He has for our lives. We know that no matter how deep the pit, how dark the night, or how insurmountable the difficulty may look, God will see us through.

Prayer

Lord, You have told me in Your Word to fight the good fight of faith, to put on the full armor of God so that I may stand against the strategies of the enemy—and win. You have told me to take the shield of faith and the sword of the Spirit and face the challenges of this life with strength and courage. You have told me to fight and win life's battles with the spirit of a conqueror. Here I am, Lord. Strengthen me by Your Spirit. Help me to fight against the forces of darkness that would try to destroy my soul. Within myself, I can do nothing, but with You and by Your Spirit, I can do all things. Give me the courage and fortitude to take my place as an overcomer of the world, a child of the Most High God. In Jesus' name I pray, amen.

Scriptures

Fight the good fight of faith, lay hold on eternal life, whereunto thou art also called, and hast professed a good profession before many witnesses.

—1 TIMOTHY 6:12

For the weapons of our warfare are not carnal, but mighty through God to the pulling down of strong holds.

—2 CORINTHIANS 10:4

For we are not fighting against flesh-and-blood enemies, but against evil rulers and authorities of the unseen world, against mighty powers in this dark world, and against evil spirits in the heavenly places. Therefore, put on every piece of God's armor so you will be able to resist the enemy in the time of evil. Then after the battle you will still be standing firm.

—EPHESIANS 6:12-13 (NLT)